Congress

Congress

Suzanne LeVert

Watts LIBRARY™

Franklin Watts
A Division of Scholastic Inc.
New York • Toronto • London • Auckland • Sydney
Mexico City • New Delhi • Hong Kong
Danbury, Connecticut

Note to readers: Definitions for words in **bold** can be found in the Glossary at the back of this book.

The illustration on the cover shows Congress in session. The photograph opposite the title page shows the Capitol building.

Photographs © 2004: AP/Wide World Photos: 38 (Dennis Cook), 41 (Charles Dharapak), 33 (Joe Marquette); Corbis Images: 6, 21, 24, 29, 32, 36, 39 (Bettmann), 5 bottom, 42, 43 (Wally McNamee), 12 (Royalty-Free); Folio, Inc./Jim LoScala: cover; Getty Images: 26 (Terry Ashe), 23 (Richard Ellis), 34 (Paul J. Richards/AFP), 31 (Mark Wilson/Newsmakers), 5 top, 16, 25 (Alex Wong), 30; Hulton | Archive/Getty Images: 10, Library of Congress via SODA: 9; PhotoEdit: 45 (Bill Aron), 46 (Paul Conklin), 17 (Tony Freeman), 22 (Jonathan Nourok), 18 (Rhoda Sidney); Visuals Unlimited/Jeff Greenberg: 2.

Library of Congress Cataloging-in-Publication Data

LeVert, Suzanne.
    Congress / Suzanne LeVert.
        p. cm. — (Watts library)
    Includes bibliographical references and index.
    ISBN 0-531-12291-3 (lib. bdg.)   0-531-16605-8 (pbk.)
    1. United States Congress—Juvenile literature. 2. Bill drafting—United States—Juvenile literature.
3. Legislation—United States—Juvenile literature. I. Title. II. Series.
JK1025.L48 2004
328.73—dc22

2004002005

Contents

Delegates at the Constitutional Convention in 1787 discussed how the government should be structured.

Creating Congress

In the spring of 1787, the cobblestone streets of Philadelphia, Pennsylvania, were full of new visitors. They came on horseback, in wagons, and on foot. They were fifty-five **delegates** from many of the states that had formed after the colonies won independence from Great Britain by winning the Revolutionary War. They gathered together to discuss ways to unify the separate states to "form a more perfect union."

The delegates met in secret at the Pennsylvania State House, known as Independence Hall, for several months. The meeting they held is called the Constitutional Convention, and the attendees are known as the founders or the framers of the Constitution. Their task was to unify the thirteen states as part of one nation and to create laws, principles, and structures to safeguard the future of the new and growing country. Some of the challenges faced by the delegates included creating ways to coin money that all states could use and to collect taxes from the citizens to support national and state programs. They also needed to establish a national army to protect citizens from foreign or domestic attacks and to manage commerce among the states. None of these activities was possible at the time. Each state had its own laws and its own form of money. The national government consisted of a small **assembly** without the power to make laws to protect all of the people or to unify the states as part of a new and free nation.

After months of discussion and compromises, the delegates produced the U.S. Constitution, a document only four pages long. In these historic four pages, the authors created a new form of government. It is called a federal republic. It divides power between the national government and the states.

The Constitution provides the national or federal government with considerable power to decide matters that affect the whole country. It also gives state governments the right to decide about certain issues that concern the individual states and their citizens. The government consists of three groups or

branches. The **legislative branch** includes the U.S. Congress, made up of the **House of Representatives** and the **Senate**, which together make the country's laws. The **executive branch** is made up of the office of the president and his or her **cabinet**, which enforce the laws. The **judicial branch** includes the Supreme Court and the federal courts, which review existing laws.

During the Constitutional Convention, delegates struggled with the question of representation in Congress and how to protect the interests of smaller states. They decided that two houses of Congress would help ensure that all citizens and

The Constitution established a new form of government called a federal republic.

This illustration shows the House of Representatives in session during the 1860s.

all states were fairly represented. In the House of Representatives, state population would determine the number of representatives. The more residents in the state, the greater the number of elected representatives the state would have. Every ten years, a national **census** would determine the states' population and determine how many seats or House memberships for each state. Representation in the Senate, however, was the same for each state. There would always be two **senators** for each state, regardless of its population.

To make sure that no one branch of government has more power than another branch, the Constitution provides an com-

The Cabinet

The president is assisted by the heads of fifteen major government departments and other important officials including the vice president. In 2002, President George W. Bush created a new department called Homeland Security to oversee the nation's safety.

plex system of checks and balances. This system requires, for example, that both the House of Representatives and the Senate agree before a **law** is passed. It gives the president the power to overturn or **veto** this very same law. At the same time, it also gives Congress the power to overturn a president's veto. The judicial branch reviews the laws that Congress passes to ensure that they are in line with the U.S. Constitution.

Congress is in charge of making laws and decisions about virtually every aspect of American life—from education to employment to national security. Its **members** are accountable to the states and the people they represent in their home state.

Congress holds its sessions in the Capitol building. The rotunda, with its huge dome, is one of the building's most distinctive features.

Chapter One

Congress in American Life

The work of senators and representatives takes place in the nation's capital, Washington, D.C., which is where all of the federal branches of government are located. High on a hill in the center of the city is the **Capitol building**, also called simply the Capitol. Elected members of Congress make the laws that guide the nation within the walls of the Capitol. One branch of the Congress, called the House of Representatives, is located in the southern wing, while the other branch, the Senate, sits in the northern wing of the Capitol. Connecting the two wings is the rotunda, a large, highly decorated round room. A huge cast-iron dome sits on top of the rotunda. And atop the dome is a statue called *Freedom*. At the base of the statue the following words are engraved: *E Pluribus Unum*, which is Latin for "Out of Many, One."

The Two Chambers of Congress

The Founding Fathers considered the creation of a national body or congress to make laws so central to the structure of a democratic republic that it takes the front-and-center position in the Constitution. It is described in the very first paragraph, called Article I, Section 1: "*All legislative Powers herein granted shall be vested in a Congress of the United States, which shall consist of a Senate and a House of Representatives.*" In this one sentence, the founders created the federal lawmaking body, the U.S. Congress, that makes the laws for the nation today.

The Congress is bicameral, which means it is made up of two houses or **chambers**. The Senate and House of Representatives work in similar ways to pass laws that affect the lives of all of the people in the country. They often work together to get the job done and must work together in order for laws to be passed.

Part of the reason to have two houses is to protect the citizens. The framers designed a bicameral system to make sure that the viewpoints of all citizens would be thoroughly represented, no matter how big or small their state. In the Senate, every state is equal regardless of its population. Every state elects two senators to Congress. In the House of Representatives, however, each state sends a number of **representatives** related to the state's population. That way, every person in each state has a representative to serve his or her interests. Another reason there are two houses is to keep a balance of power. One house keeps an eye on the other house, and both must agree before either can take action on **legislation**, or laws.

The Constitution gave Congress a broad range of powers, including collecting taxes, borrowing and spending money, and providing for national defense. It also has the power to declare war and to **ratify** treaties. Congress also approves appointments to national offices, such as federal judges and cabinet members, and makes other laws it considers "necessary and proper."

Congress in American Life

According to the Constitution, Congress must assemble at least once every year, at noon on the third day of January, unless changed by law. A term of Congress lasts for two years, starting in January of the year after the biennial (every two years) election of members. Since the first Congress gathered, each Congress has been numbered in order. The Congress in **session** in 2003 was the 108th Congress. A Congress is made up of two sessions, one during the first year and one during the second year of a Congress.

The Democratic and Republican Parties control Congress.

Upper and Lower Houses

The idea for a congress with two houses had its roots in the British system, which includes a lower house called the House of Parliament, whose members are elected by the people. Its upper house is the House of Lords, whose members are selected by their peers or, in the past, by nobles. The framers believed that the House should be "the grand depository of the democratic principle of the government." Right from the start, House members were elected directly by the people of their states. Until 1913, state legislators, rather than the state's citizens, elected their senators.

15

Members of the U.S. House of Representatives are sworn in by the Speaker of the House during opening day ceremonies the 108th Congress.

The party with the most members in a chamber of Congress is the **majority** party, and the party with the fewest members is called the **minority** party. Independent party and other smaller, third-party candidates run for office and are elected to Congress as well.

While state governments make laws that specifically affect the lives of the people of their states, Congress focuses on the issues that affect the lives of the people of the entire country. They include national defense, education, automobile safety, agriculture, civil rights, housing, employment, poverty, the environment, and numerous other topics.

Congress also decides how to spend money from the national **budget**. The budget begins with the president, who submits a draft budget to the House of Representatives. The House then works its way through the budget, adding or

16

deleting items as it sees fit. Although the president is a very powerful figure in the government, it is Congress that has the final say on the budget. More money for after-school programs? More funds for cancer research? Less money for unemployment benefits? Increased or decreased funding for the military? Choices like these, made every day by members of Congress, are important ones that have an impact on the everyday lives of Americans.

The job of Congress and its role in American life and government can be confusing and a bit mysterious to ordinary citizens. Congress is, after all, a large government agency with many duties, offices, committees, and responsibilities. So it's natural that people might have lots of questions about how Congress works. How many people serve in each house? How are they elected? How do they work together? How do they pass laws? And how can the people make sure their senators and representatives are doing a good job? Let's take a closer look at the inner workings of each chamber of Congress.

Members of Congress have many responsibilities, including helping to determine how the government spends its money and what programs, such as after-school classes, will receive funds.

17

Every ten years, the government conducts a census to determine how many people are living in the United States. The results of this poll may affect how many representatives each state has in the House.

Chapter Two

The House of Representatives

Since the first census in 1790, politicians have argued over the results that have come from the process. If the population of a state changes, it may gain or lose "seats" or memberships in the House. Furthermore, because all representatives in a state must serve an equal number of people in the state, the state must refigure its districts so each one is equal in population if the population changes. Another result of a census that indicates a state's population has changed is called

To Be a Representative

Representatives must be at least twenty-five years old, U.S. citizens for at least seven years, and residents of their states.

redistricting, which is the refiguring of the area represented. Representatives can find themselves running for election in a district that had been loyal to an opposing party's candidate. Sometimes, whole districts are eliminated. Arguments about the fairness of the census and the redistricting maps have led to bitter battles and accusations of **gerrymandering**.

The term "gerrymandering" is used to describe the redrawing of congressional districts to give one political party an advantage. The practice has been ruled illegal, but the political parties sometimes try to bend the rules, redrawing boundaries to improve their chances of winning. States often redraw the congressional districts to make sure each district has an equal number of **constituents**.

The first federal Congress **convened** in 1789 with one hundred representatives, with each representative serving about 30,000 people in their states. House membership had

Call It a Gerrymander!

According to some accounts, the Massachusetts state legislature presented a new congressional **district** to Governor Elbridge Gerry in 1810. The map was strangely shaped. Areas that supported the Federalist Party were grouped together. The remaining districts, made up of citizens who supported the rival party called the Democratic-Republican Party, formed a figure that resembled a salamander. The editor for a Federalist newspaper was so angered that Governor Gerry had approved the plan, that he shouted, "Salamander! Call it a Gerrymander!" The paper published a cartoon of the map, adding wings, claws, and a salamander head to the shape of the Democratic-Republican Party districts.

increased to 435 by 1911. In 1929, Congress decided to limit membership to 435. Since the population continues to grow in many states, representatives serve the needs of an ever-growing number of people. Today, a member of the House represents about 650,000 constituents. There is some talk of increasing the number of House members in the future so that they can better serve a smaller number of constituents.

The state with the largest number of people is California. It has fifty-three representatives. Several states with small populations have only one representative for the entire state. Four delegates serve the U.S. territories of American Samoa, Guam, the U.S. Virgin Islands, and the District of Columbia, and a **resident commissioner** represents the territory of Puerto Rico. Although these delegates cannot vote on legislation, they serve on committees, where they are able to vote and help shape new laws.

The first Congress was much smaller than the Congress we have today.

The Role of the House

The House of Representatives is often called the "People's House" because its members are linked to the people who live in their districts. Representatives serve two-year terms, so they must be in tune with their constituents' views, which can

Representatives spend a lot of their time trying to help their constituents, or the people they represent.

change quickly in that time. Representatives juggle numerous duties, serving the interests of their constituents, their states, and the nation.

Casework, or working on behalf of individual constituents, is a big part of a representative's job. A constituent can turn to his or her representative to help with personal or community issues, such as immigration or citizenship problems, public-housing disputes, or welfare benefits. Representatives cannot solve all problems, but they can expect to work hard for their constituents.

The House has a number of special responsibilities and powers granted through the Constitution. It has the power to create all laws related to the raising and spending of money. The House is also charged with the power to impeach, or bring charges against a president or government official

House Rules

The House of Representatives is a decidedly democratic institution. It elects its own leaders and creates its own rules and procedures. In order to pass legislation, a majority of representatives must agree. With hundreds of representatives, there are many rules, procedures, and debates. At the start of the day, a representative may speak for one minute on a topic of his or her choice. A **five-minute rule** is in effect when a representative wishes to propose an amendment or a change to a proposed bill. And for the most important issues, majority and minority leaders are given an hour or an agreed upon time for debate, which can be divided up among other members.

accused of wrongdoing. If the House votes to impeach an official, the Senate holds a formal hearing or trial. Another important job of House members is to decide who will be president if no one presidential candidate wins a majority of electoral votes. The Senate decides who will be vice president if no candidate for that position wins a majority of votes. In addition, the highest-ranking House member, the **Speaker** of the House, is next in line to become president should both the president and the vice president die or leave office.

In 1998, the House Judiciary Committee held hearings to determine whether impeachment proceedings should begin against President Bill Clinton.

Leaders of the House

In both the Senate and the House, several key officials are in charge of congressional proceedings. In the House, these include the Speaker of the House, who is elected by the majority party during a congressional session. The Speaker makes the rules for proceedings, calls on representatives who wish to

A Woman's Place Is in the House

In 1916, Jeanette Rankin became the first woman to serve in the House—and this was before women had the right to vote! In 1968, Shirley Chisholm became the first African-American woman elected to the House. Since 1916, there have been close to two hundred representatives who are women. Today, about sixty-two women serve as representatives.

In addition, other minority representation has grown, though slowly. In 2003, thirty-seven African-Americans, twenty-two Hispanic Americans, and four Asian Americans serve in the House.

speak, and sets the schedule for introducing and voting on bills. Assisting the Speaker is the majority leader and majority **whip**, who help round up support and votes for his or her party's legislation. The leadership for the minority party includes the minority leader and minority whip, who also work to get support and count the votes for their party's point of view and legislation. House leaders have a great deal of power over the legislation that representatives actually get to vote on. This is different than the Senate, where any one of the one hundred lawmakers has strong individual powers.

Committees play important roles in congressional proceedings by investigating issues, hearing testimony from experts and other interested parties, creating bills, and advising party members. There are about nineteen formal committees in the House and sixteen in the Senate. The number of committees can vary from session to session. There are also more than one hundred smaller committees and party **caucuses**. Caucuses are informal groups of people who belong to the same political party or who hold similar interests. Lawmakers usually serve on a number of committees and subcommittees and are free to join caucuses.

The House and the Senate are considered equal halves of Congress. There are some differences between the two chambers in terms of rules, terms of office, and primary responsibilities. Just as the House has certain responsibilities and powers, the Senate has specific powers provided by the Constitution.

James Wright Jr., Thomas Foley, Newt Gingrich, and Dennis Hastert (left to right) have all held the position of Speaker of the House.

Senator Robert Byrd was first elected senator in 1958 and has represented the state of West Virginia for more than forty years.

Chapter Three

The Senate

On June 10, 1964, Senator Robert Byrd spoke for fourteen hours and thirteen minutes on the **floor** of the Senate. The senator's all-night speech aimed to stop **debate** on a civil rights **bill** so the Senate could not vote on it and it would not be passed. This tactic is called a **filibuster**. Other senators had already used filibusters several times to prevent civil rights legislation, but before there had never been enough votes to end the filibuster, a process called **cloture**. This time was different.

The Senate leadership called for a vote to end the filibuster. When the clerk

Filibusters: For the Record

The point of a filibuster is to keep talking so that no one else can. The speaker may not sit down, stop talking, or leave the chamber. In 1935, Senator Huey Long stayed on his feet for fifteen hours and thirty minutes, offering his opinions on a wide range of subjects, reading from the Bible, and even providing his recipe for fried oysters. Senator Strom Thurmond holds the record at twenty-four hours and eighteen minutes, filibustering the same bill that Senator Byrd had: the Civil Rights Act of 1964. The great filibusters in the Senate are rare events today as Senate leaders employ other methods to cut off debate or to kill bills.

came to Senator Clair Engle, there was no sound. Suffering from a brain tumor, the senator could not speak. He did, however, lift his arm and point at his eye, indicating an "eye" (an "aye" or yes vote). The Senate passed the Civil Rights Act of 1964 nine days later, a great step forward for equality and civil rights in the United States.

Creating the Senate

In creating the Senate, the framers borrowed not only from the English system but also from that of the Roman Republic. In Latin, *senatus* means "council of elders." In ancient Rome, the Senate was the highest state council. From the start, the U.S. Senate was a small, carefully selected group. The first Senate included only twenty-six members, chosen by their state's legislatures. U.S. senators were not elected by state popular vote until 1913, when Congress enacted an amendment to the Constitution.

The framers of the Constitution gave the House the responsibility to serve the interests of the people of their states. As a balance, they provided the Senate with the responsibility of looking after both state and national interests. In order to create a Senate made up of experienced thinkers and politicians, the framers required that senators be at least thirty years old and a U.S. citizen for at least nine years. Life experience, they hoped, would ensure "greater extent of information and stability of character."

Today, there are one hundred voting members of the Senate, two from every state. They must be residents of the state in which they run, and they must serve for six years. They are not, however, all elected at the same time. Instead, one-third of the Senate is elected or reelected every two years. This schedule keeps a revolving group of senators in service for six years but still keeps them in touch with current state and national issues.

Trailblazing Senators

The vast majority of Senators remain male and Caucasian, but members of other backgrounds have increased over time. In 1922, Rebecca Latimer Felton, at age eighty-seven, was the first woman appointed to the Senate. In 1932, Hattie Wyatt Caraway became the first woman elected to the Senate. Since then, thirty-three women have served in the Senate, with fourteen serving as of 2003.

People of African-American, Asian American, Hispanic American, and Native American descent have made some progress in increasing the diversity of Senate representation. One early trailblazer was Hiram R. Revels (above), the first African-American to serve in the Senate in 1870.

The Power to Impeach

Impeachment is a congressional accusation of a crime by a president or high official. The House brings the charges, called the Articles of Impeachment. They are then sent to the Senate for a formal trial. If a two-thirds majority of senators return a guilty verdict, the official is removed from office. Richard Nixon resigned before his impeachment trial, leaving Andrew Jackson and Bill Clinton as the only two U.S. presidents to undergo impeachment trials in the Senate. Neither was found guilty, and both served out their presidential terms.

The Role of the Senate

Senators create and pass legislation, such as laws that promote fair practices in business and organizations and that protect individual privacy. They also work on laws that support farmers, provide aid to the needy and others in national and international emergencies, and fund programs in the arts and sciences. The Senate and the House work together in many of these areas, and both must agree before a bill becomes a law.

The Constitution grants the Senate certain special powers and responsibilities, just as it does to the House. The Senate oversees **impeachment** trials of presidents and other federal officials. To remove a president from office, two-thirds of the Senate must reach a guilty verdict of wrongdoing, defined in the Constitution as "treason, bribery, or other high crimes and misdemeanors."

Another key Senate responsibility is to advise the president about issues of national and international importance. Although both houses of Congress have joint power to declare war, the Senate is responsible for approving international treaties. The Senate also votes on presidential nominations of key officials, such as ambassadors, Supreme Court justices, and cabinet officials.

The Senate Judiciary Committee conducts a confirmation hearing to determine whether to approve the president's choice for U.S. attorney general.

Senate Leaders and Rules

The vice president of the United States serves as president of the Senate. The vice president often has many other duties, so that job often falls to the **president pro tempore**, the highest-ranking senator from the majority party. As in the House, the Senate's daily scheduling and business falls to leaders of political parties, with the majority party taking control. In the Senate, they are called floor leaders, and they include the majority leader and majority whip and the minority leader and minority whip. And as in the House, much of the preliminary work on legislation is done in committees. There are

President Harry S. Truman meets with the president pro tempore and the Speaker of the House.

about sixteen Senate committees and more than triple that number of smaller committees, which focus on specific issues.

Like members of the House, senators follow certain rules when presenting a bill for consideration, requesting to speak, or debating an issue. Floor leaders in the Senate are allotted the most amount of speaking time during debate. In general, Senate rules are much more relaxed than those in the House. Everyone has an equal voice, including those belonging to the minority party. Despite the senators' outwardly polite behavior, there often are hard-fought battles waged on the floor of the Senate. Some of these disputes have not been as civilized as U.S. citizens might have imagined from their elected officials. During the 1800s, some arguments were settled by duels, gunshots, and fistfights.

Tom Daschle, former majority leader, holds up a bill under consideration.

Today, civilized members of Congress work together to ensure the security, safety, and well-being of all Americans. The legislative process—from proposing a bill to passing a law—is long and rather complex. It requires expert scheduling, knowledge, strategy, and cooperation from all branches of the government. This procedure takes place in Congress.

Christopher Reeve and U.S. Representative James Langevin hold a press conference to discuss The Christopher Reeve Paralysis Act of 2003.

Chapter Four

From a Bill to a Law

In May of 2003, Christopher Reeve, paralyzed from a fall from a horse, came before Congress to voice his support for The Christopher Reeve Paralysis Act of 2003. Identical versions of the proposal were supported or sponsored by four representatives and two senators. This proposed bill would expand funding from several national health agencies for research efforts and would increase services to improve the quality of life for people living with paralysis. Reeve is very

Seventy-seventh Congress of the United States of America;

At the First Session

Begun and held at the City of Washington on Friday, the third
day of January, one thousand nine hundred and forty-one

JOINT RESOLUTION

Declaring that a state of war exists between the Imperial Government
of Japan and the Government and the people of the United States
and making provisions to prosecute the same.

Whereas the Imperial Government of Japan has committed unpro-
voked acts of war against the Government and the people of the
United States of America: Therefore be it

*Resolved by the Senate and House of Representatives of the
United States of America in Congress assembled,* That the state of
war between the United States and the Imperial Government of
Japan which has thus been thrust upon the United States is hereby
formally declared; and the President is hereby authorized and
directed to employ the entire naval and military forces of the United
States and the resources of the Government to carry on war against
the Imperial Government of Japan; and, to bring the conflict to a
successful termination, all of the resources of the country are hereby
pledged by the Congress of the United States.

Speaker of the House of Representatives.

*This joint resolution
was used to declare war
on Japan during
World War II.*

hopeful that both houses of Congress and the president will approve the bill. It is too early at this time to tell what may happen to this bill, but let's look at how a bill such as this might become a law.

The Journey from Bill to Law

Tracing the process of passing a law in Congress is a tricky, winding path. The road can lead to a number of destinations or even to dead ends.

Congress acts on several types of legislation, including **resolutions** and bills. A **joint** resolution can extend emergency appropriations, provide funding for the government or programs, or propose **amendments** to the Constitution. It requires approval from both houses and the president and has the force of law. A concurrent resolution requires acceptance from both houses but not from the president. Congress uses a concurrent resolution to amend rules followed by both houses or to communicate opinions of Congress to the public. A simple resolution focuses on issues affecting one house of Congress, including revising its rules, formally acknowledging the death of a member, or offering opinions about international affairs. A simple resolution does not require the approval of both houses or that of the president. Neither concurrent nor simple resolutions have the same power as a law.

The most common and important form of congressional legislation is a bill. A bill may be introduced by either the House or the Senate. To become a law, also called an act or a statute, both houses of Congress and the president must approve the bill. Only members of Congress can propose a bill. When nonmembers, such as individuals or organizations, wish to introduce legislation, they must gain the support of a member of Congress. That person is the bill's sponsor. The first official action taken is to number the bill and label it either H.R. (from the House of Representatives) or S. (from the Senate).

Committees and Subcommittees

Once a bill is introduced in Congress by its sponsors, it is usually referred to particular congressional committees. There are about 250 standing committees and subcommittees in Congress. In both houses, party leaders decide which committees their members will join. They also decide to which committee a bill will be sent. It is an important job since committees decide which bills will be reviewed and supported. With thousands of bills introduced every session, this can be a lengthy process.

One route a bill can take is to a full committee, which puts the bill on its **calendar** for consideration. After review, the

The Hopper

The hopper is a mahogany box located on the floor of the House. Representatives place the bill, with their signature, in the hopper. In the Senate, a senator usually presents a bill to one of the clerks, usually without comment. Sometimes a senator may rise and make an official statement about the bill.

Members of a committee discuss an energy bill.

committee decides the next step, usually based on what chance it has to be approved by Congress. A committee may decide to take no action, in which case the bill goes no further. It is "dead." Or the committee may choose to study the bill further before taking a vote.

Another possible path is for the committee to refer the bill to a committee or a subcommittee to study and conduct **hearings** on its merits. The subcommittee may decide to take no further action, in which case the bill is dead. Or the subcommittee may choose to make changes to the bill—called "marking up" the bill—before sending it to the full committee.

If the subcommittee submits a report to the full committee, then the full committee does one of two things. It conducts more studies and hearings or it votes on the subcommittee's recommendations, including its own **markups**. It then "orders a bill reported," recommending or not recommending, the bill to the House or Senate. The full committee may then hold a markup of its own, after which it writes a comprehensive report, stating the bill's purpose, the position of the president, and any criticisms that committee members may have.

Often, bills must go through this process in several

different committees claiming **jurisdiction** over the legislation. This takes time and also means that the final version of the bill may not look much like the original.

Floor Action

Finally, this bill is out of committee and on its way back to the chamber where it started and placed on the appropriate calendar. The House has several different types of calendars, managed by the Speaker, while the Senate uses a single calendar.

When the bill finally comes before the appropriate house of Congress, members of that house then have a chance to review it among themselves. As discussed previously, the House of Representatives has stricter guidelines and limits discussion, while the Senate allows more time for all members to weigh in on decisions. After debate has ended, the members of the House or the Senate vote on the bill. If it is defeated,

In the chamber, senators debate a military training bill in 1940.

the bill is dead. If it is approved by a majority of members, the bill gets to go through the entire process again in the other chamber of Congress. Sometimes, to save time, identical versions of proposed legislation may be introduced in the House and the Senate at the same time.

If the second chamber also approves the bill, but makes minor, easily addressed alterations, the bill returns to home base to make sure members of that house approve the changes. However, if the second chamber makes major changes, a **conference committee** made up of members of both houses work together on the differences between the two versions. If they cannot agree, the bill is dead. If they do agree, they submit a report of their work. Both houses then vote to accept or reject the committee's "conference report." If accepted, then the bill is not yet a law. There is one more step.

After passing both houses, Congress presents the bill to the president. If the president votes to accept the bill, then the bill becomes the law of the land. The bill also becomes law if the president does not take any action on the bill for ten days

while Congress is in session. If the president takes no action while Congress is not in session, the bill dies as a result of a **pocket veto**. If the president vetoes the bill while Congress is in session, then Congress can overturn or **override** the veto if two-thirds of its members agree. Then the bill becomes law.

This conference committee met to discuss Medicare legislation.

After the successful passage of a law, it is possible that the Supreme Court may decide that the bill Congress and the president passed does not conform to the principles of the Constitution. Then the Court rules the law unconstitutional.

Undergoing such a long and studied process, it is not surprising that only about 5 percent of bills become laws. The checks and balances outlined in the Constitution may seem to slow down the legislative process, but they serve to ensure that no one branch of government has more say than another about the laws that govern the nation.

During the Vietnam War era, people protested outside of the Capitol building to let members of Congress know that they wanted to stop the war.

Chapter Five

Making Congress Work

Congress works for all the people of the United States. The laws it passes are intended to protect civil rights, privacy, and safety. Congress also decides how clean the environment should be, when and how to react to violence in the nation, and how much tax money will be collected. Not everyone agrees with the decisions our government makes. Often, citizens feel so strongly that they organize campaigns or protests to stop certain legislation. The Constitution gives us the right to express our opinions. It is the duty of people to work to change the laws they disagree with and to enact new laws to make the United States a better country.

Each individual can work to make a difference. Not all efforts succeed, of course. The passage of a law depends on a number of circumstances and events, including the political parties that control Congress, the viewpoints of the president, and the amount of public pressure. Sometimes laws are passed because of pressure from **lobbyists**, who represent individuals, organizations, or private businesses that attempt to influence members of Congress to consider particular legislation. Ordinary citizens can lobby for change and celebrities, like Christopher Reeve and others, can often speed up the legislative process a bit.

Getting Involved

How can you get involved? First, it is important to understand what Congress does and how it works. Find out the names of your U.S. senators and your congressional representative by searching the Internet. There are a number of interesting Web sites that contain details of recent, current, and upcoming legislation, and the names, addresses, and Web sites of senators and representatives. The Senate's Web site is especially rich with current and historical information.

Writing to your senator or congressional representative is a good way to begin a dialogue about the issues you care about and the actions that Congress has taken or is considering.

Often a class of students joins together to communicate with members of Congress, which may even increase the chance of a personal visit! It is important to figure out just what you want to say or suggest in your communication. It is equally important that your letter or email be respectful, polite, and to the point.

Writing a letter is one of the ways that you can express your opinions and concerns to your congressional representative.

Visiting Congress

Do you want to be inspired by government and Congress? A visit to Washington, D.C., and a tour of the Capitol building will surely do just that. Thomas Jefferson predicted correctly that the building would captivate everyone who saw it. It is a massive structure, containing some 540 rooms and 850 doorways. The rooms are ornate, designed with bronze panels, marble statues, and beautifully painted domed ceilings. The architecture is stunning and the historic artifacts fascinating. The Capitol is like a little city, with its own post office,

A group of students meet with their congressional representative during a class trip to Washington, D.C.

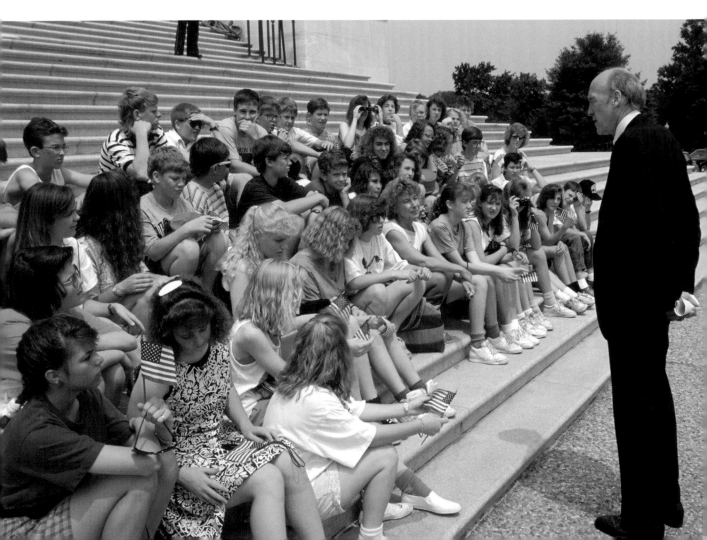

barbershop, banks, power plant, and even a private subway system.

The Capitol is open to the public during certain days and is well worth a visit. The chambers of Congress are located in wings off the rotunda. Many proceedings and hearings are open to the public for viewing. You may even schedule an appointment to meet with your senator or representative during your trip. If you can't make it to the nation's capitol, C-SPAN broadcasts congressional proceedings every day, including debates, hearings, and speeches.

It's up to you, and all Americans, to keep informed about the work that Congress does and the issues it acts upon so that we can help keep the spirit of democracy alive through our active participation.

Timeline

1774	The Continental Congress is created as the colonies prepare for the American Revolution.
1789	The first U.S. Congress is created by the U.S. Constitution and convenes in New York City.
1796	George Washington gives his farewell speech to members of Congress. Since 1893, the reading of his 7,641-word address has become an annual Senate tradition on or around the date of his birthday, February 22.
1800	Congress convenes for the first time in its new quarters, the Capitol building in Washington, D.C.
1816	The Senate creates the first permanent congressional committees.
1837	The Senate elects the vice president, Richard Mentor Johnson, since no candidate received a majority of electoral votes.
1861–1865	Southern states are not represented in Congress during the Civil War.
1865–1870	Lawmakers from the southern states rejoin the Congress.
1870	The first African-American, Hiram R. Revels, is elected to the Senate.
1912	Passage of the Seventeenth Amendment provides direct, popular elections of senators.
1916	The first woman, Jeannette Rankin, is appointed to the House.
1919	The Senate rejects membership in the League of Nations.
1922	The first woman, Rebecca Felton, is appointed to the Senate.

1932	World War I veterans and their families go to Washington, D.C., to demand bonus pay promised by Congress for their service. Some 20,000 people camp out around the city. In July, troops storm their camps, set the camps on fire, and drive them from the city. Later, the unemployed veterans accept work under programs created by President Roosevelt.
1932	Hattie Wyatt Caraway becomes the first woman elected to the Senate.
1938	The House establishes the House Un-American Activities Committee (HUAC) to investigate citizens believed to be unpatriotic, especially those involved in groups such as the Communist or Socialist Parties. Targets include government workers, artists, writers, and labor leaders.
1948	Margaret Chase Smith becomes the first woman to serve in both the Senate and the House.
1950	A crime committee headed by Senator Estes Kefauver holds public hearings to investigate organized crime in the United States. It is the first hearing to receive extensive television coverage.
1954	Senator Joseph McCarthy chairs HUAC hearings into alleged communist membership and activities, targeting writers, filmmakers, and others. McCarthy is later discredited.
1964	The Civil Rights Act of 1964 is passed.
1968	Shirley Chisholm is the first African-American woman elected to the House.
1972	Barbara Jordan and Andrew Young become the first southern African-Americans elected to Congress since the 1800s.
1973	The Watergate hearings are conducted, investigating a break-in at the Watergate office building complex, used by the Democratic National Committee, by burglars linked to President Nixon's reelection committee in 1972.

1974	The House conducts impeachment hearings to investigate President Nixon's involvement in the "Watergate" scandal. The president resigns before the House votes for impeachment.
1979	C-SPAN begins cable TV broadcasts of the House of Representatives.
1986	The Senate votes to allow C-SPAN coverage.
1998	President Bill Clinton is impeached by the House. He is later acquitted by the Senate.
2002	Department of Homeland Security is created to oversee national safety following terrorist attacks on the United States in 2001.
2003	The United States Leadership against HIV/AIDS, Tuberculosis, and Malaria Act of 2003 is passed to provide financial assistance to people suffering from or vulnerable to these diseases around the world.

Glossary

amendment—a change to a bill or document

assembly—a meeting

bill—a proposed law. A bill can originate in either house but can only be introduced by members of Congress

budget—a report of estimates of government revenues (money coming in to the government) and expenditures (money to be spent by the government) that Congress receives from the president for revision and approval

cabinet—an executive department that works with and advises the president on important national and international issues. The president appoints the heads or secretaries of each department.

calendar—a schedule for Congressional tasks to be completed, such as bills or resolutions for committee consideration. The House and Senate schedule work on separate calendars.

Capitol building—the main structure for the House of Representatives and the Senate, located in Washington, D.C.

casework—the work or help a representative provides for an individual constituent

caucus—an informal meeting of members who share interests, positions, or political parties. The largest caucuses are the Democratic and Republican caucuses.

census—a study undertaken to count all the people living in the United States

chamber—the place in the Senate where senators meet as a group, and the place in the House where representatives meet as a group

cloture—a Senate rule that limits debate to end a filibuster

committee—a group of senators or representatives who discuss and investigate specific issues and prepare legislation for their party for voting. There are about 250 congressional committees and subcommittees.

conference committee—a group of five senators and five representatives who meet to resolve differences when the two houses approve different versions of the same bill

constituent—a person represented by a member of Congress

convene—to come together in a body or group for a meeting or gathering

debate—to present points of view and listen to opposing arguments about a bill

delegate—a representative from a U.S. territory or the District of Columbia. Delegates cannot vote on the floor but can vote in committees.

district—the geographic area of a state served by a representative

executive branch—part of the U.S. government made up of the president, the president's cabinet, and other high officials

filibuster—a tactic to delay or stop senators from voting on a bill

five-minute rule—in the House, a member supporting a change or amendment to a bill may speak for five minutes. A member opposing the amendment may then speak for five minutes.

floor—the whole chamber of the House or the Senate where members debate or vote on a bill

gerrymandering—the term for changing congressional districts for the sole benefit of a political party; a practice that is illegal

hearing—a meeting of a committee to study and listen to testimony on particular issues or to question the president's policies

House of Representatives—one of the two chambers of the U.S. Congress

impeachment—the penalty for wrongdoing by the president or other high officials. The House issues Articles of Impeachment. The Senate holds impeachment trials to determine the accused guilt or innocence and can trigger removal from office.

joint—involving both chambers of Congress. A joint committee has members from both the Senate and the House; a joint resolution is one that both houses support. A joint meeting is when both houses meet when a dignitary, or important person, is speaking. A joint session is when both houses assemble to hear a president's address or to count electoral votes during a presidential election.

judicial branch—the part of the government made up of the Supreme Court and the federal courts

jurisdiction—the power and right to interpret and apply the law

law—a legal rule governing actions or procedures. In Congress, laws begin as proposed bills. When both houses pass the bill and the president signs it, the bill becomes a law. Laws are also called acts or statutes.

legislation—the laws that Congress or other legislators pass

legislative branch—the lawmaking part of the U.S. government; the Congress

lobbyist—a person who meets with legislators to advocate for certain legislation

majority—the greater number. In Congress, a majority of members must pass a bill or a law. The majority party is the political party with the greater number of members in Congress.

markup—a congressional committee meeting where changes in a bill's language are debated and voted on

member—an elected official who serves in the House. The term can also refer to one who serves in the Senate, as in "a member of Congress."

minority—the lesser number. In Congress, the minority party's work is led by the minority leader and the minority whip.

override—when legislators overrule or overturn a veto by the president (or in states, by the governor)

pocket veto—when a bill is vetoed or killed by the president after no action is taken by the president while Congress is not in session

president pro tempore—the official who is in charge of the Senate when the president of the Senate (the vice president of the United States) is not present

ratify—to officially approve

representative—a member of the House of Representatives

resident commissioner—the representative from Puerto Rico, who has limited voting privileges and who serves for four years

resolution—a written opinion or expression from a member of the House or Senate

Senate—one of two chambers of the U.S. Congress

senator—a member of the Senate

session—a period of time when Congress meets. Each two-year term of Congress includes two sessions.

Speaker—the chief officer of the House of Representatives

veto—rejection of a bill by the president that may be over-turned by a two-thirds vote in both houses of Congress

whip—the member of both the majority and minority parties in both houses whose job it is to round up party support for legislation and other congressional activity

To Find Out More

Books

January, Brendan. *The Presidency*. Danbury, CT: Franklin Watts, 2004.

January, Brendan. *The Supreme Court*. Danbury, CT: Franklin Watts, 2004.

Silverberg, David. *Congress for Dummies*. New York: John Wiley & Sons, 2002.

Stein, R. Conrad. *Washington, D.C.* Danbury, CT: Children's Press, 2004.

Organizations and Online Sites

Ben's Guide to U.S. Government for Kids
http://bensguide.gpo.gov
This site provides students with an excellent overview of Congress and other government agencies and departments.

Kids in the House: The Office of the Clerk
http://clerkkids.house.gov
This interactive, educational site explores the role of the House and of the clerk.

The U.S. House of Representatives
http://www.house.gov
Here you can find historical data, roll call votes on legislation, the names of your representatives, and the addresses of members' Web sites.

The U.S. Senate
http://www.senate.gov
Here you can find the names of your senators and the addresses of members' own Web sites. The site also includes spectacular "virtual tours" of the Capitol, from its initial construction to its present structure.

A Note on Sources

There are scores of books and other material available about Congress. Some are a bit technical, with plenty of detail about the inner workings of both houses, and others are engaging first-person accounts from members who have served in the House or the Senate. I found *Congress for Dummies* entertaining, easy to follow, and informative. The memoirs of Massachusetts Representative Tip O'Neill, who served in the Massachusetts legislature and later in the House of Representatives, are lively and engaging. Serving from 1953–1987, his House career included positions as majority leader, majority whip, and Speaker of the House.

I found the government's Internet sites to be invaluable in researching both the history of Congress and its current, day-to-day activities. You can also read two congressional publications online. *The Congressional Record* is a daily account of House and Senate activities, including debates, speeches, remarks, and vote tallies. The second, *The Congressional Quarterly*, is a weekly guide to activities in Congress.

If you enjoy political news, C-SPAN was created just for you. C-SPAN is a public service created by the cable television industry that broadcasts live coverage of House and Senate proceedings, as well as political commentaries.

Nothing beats talking one-to-one with a member of Congress. You might be surprised to learn that representatives and senators often take time from their busy schedules to meet with students and other interested citizens. This is not so astonishing since the citizens of their districts are their constituents—they work for us!

—*Suzanne LeVert*

Index

Numbers in *italics* indicate illustrations.

About the Author

Suzanne LeVert is the author of more than twenty nonfiction books for young readers, including several about the U.S. government. She is a graduate of New York University and Tulane Law School. She lives in New Orleans, Louisiana, where she is an assistant district attorney for Orleans Parish.